MAD'S

Dave Berg

LOOKS AT

LIVING

written and drawn
by DAVE BERG

**WARNER
PAPERBACK
LIBRARY**

A Warner Communications Company

WARNER PAPERBACK LIBRARY EDITION
First Printing: November, 1973

Copyright © 1973 by Dave Berg and E.C. Publications, Inc. All rights
reserved. No part of this book may be reproduced without permission. For
information address E.C. Publications, Inc., 485 Madison Avenue, New York,
N.Y. 10022

Title "MAD" used with permission of its owner,
E.C. Publications, Inc.

This Warner Paperback Library Edition is published by
arrangement with E.C. Publications, Inc.

**Warner Paperback Library is a division of Warner Books, Inc.,
75 Rockefeller Plaza, New York, N.Y. 10019.**

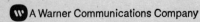 A Warner Communications Company

LIVING AND LEARNING

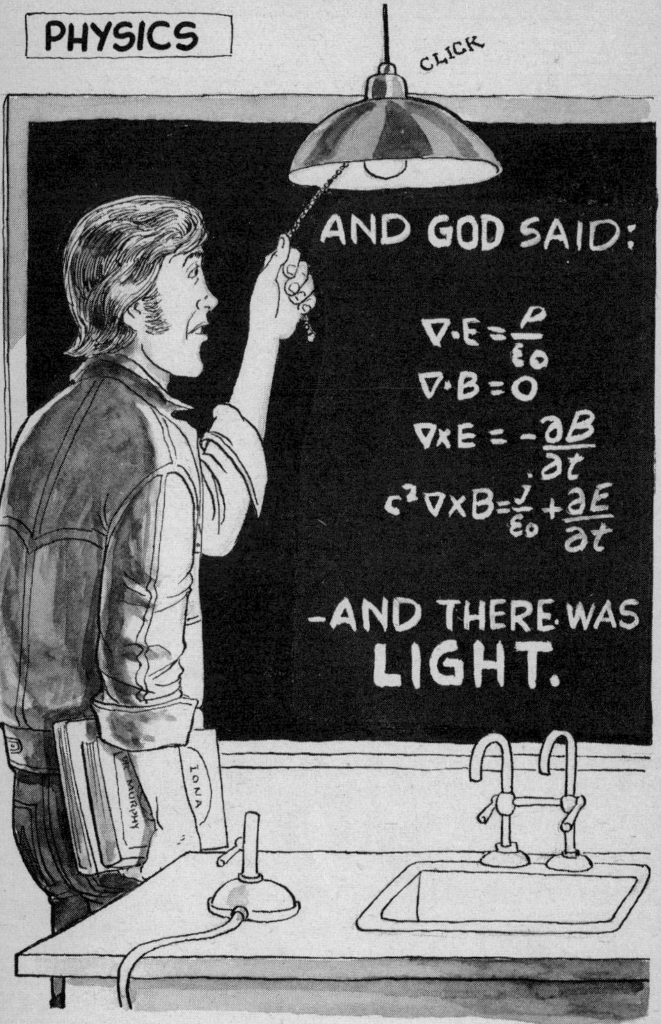

THE PAUSE THAT DEPRESSES

INSTANT REPLAY

BED AND BORED

Boredom is one of the great enemies of mankind. Nature abhors monotony like it abhors a vacuum.

The anatomy of Boredom
monotony

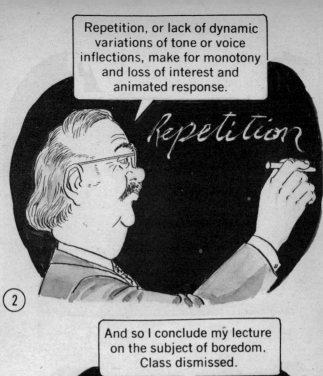

STUDENT BODY

SUBJECT TO CHANGE

HOME "REMEDY"

Those darn **coddling parents** of mine made me go to a **commuting college**. Which means a big trip everyday.

What the heck for?

(1)

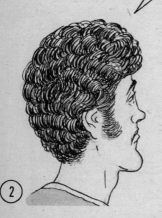

They're afraid that if I lived in a dorm, I'd be involved in a **pot party every night**.

(2)

UNKINDEST CUT OF ALL

ROAD SCHOLAR

Today in Sunday School we're going to learn about the parable of the good Samaritan. It's about a man who was walking along the road when he was beaten and robbed. All other travelers just passed him by until the good Samaritan came along.

①

LIVING AND LOVING

Lovers'
Lane

TRUTH AND CONSEQUENCES

That Gloria I was going steady with, did she turn out to be a **dirty, rotten, TWO TIMING WITCH.**

(1)

You should have heard her when she poured out all that **phony sugary emotions** while we both **swore faithfulness** to **each other.**

(2)

KISS OR TELL

CHASTE MAKES WASTE

There's that Regina Kaputnik. Keep away from her. She has a **terrible reputation.**

(1)

Her morals are a throwback to some distant horrible dark age. She's an **embarrassment to the entire college.**

(2)

LOVE SICKNESS

MAIL CHAUVINIST

PRAISE UNWORTHY

1

2

SOLID STATE MATE

That's even **better** than a doctor. A T.V. repairman gets **more** money for a house call.

SWINGING IN THE BRAIN

NOTES TO YOU

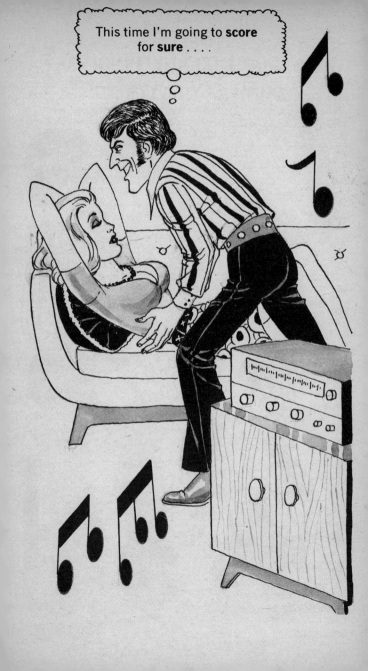

BUGGING OUT

THE WEIGH TO ROMANCE

PHOTO-FINISH

BRIDE AND GLOOM

It was the emotion—sob—in the way you—sob—delivered your lines—sob—in the ceremony. It got me—sob—right here where I live—sob—
2

RICE TO THE OCCASION

Isn't that **disgusting?** After going through the ceremony of **Holy** Matrimony in a **House of GOD**, they **defile** it all by then going through the **pagan fertility rite of throwing rice.**

①

(2)

(3)

LIVING TOGETHER

YESTERDAZE

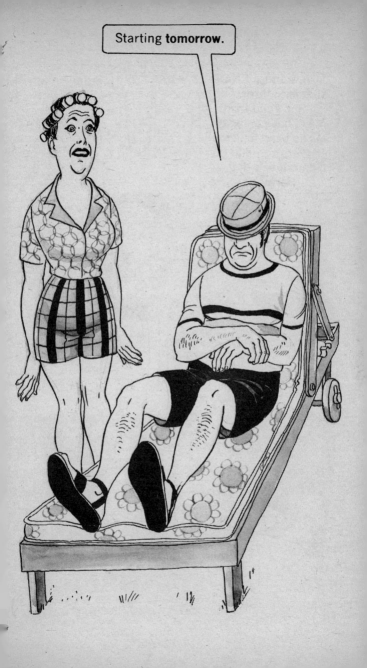

IT'S A DOG'S WIFE

THE CALL OF THE MILD

Hi Nick, this is Jerry. Judy and I have been stuck in the house for so long with the baby, we decided for a change to go out tonight. We were wondering if your daughter can baby sit for us.

You're going out? And you didn't ask us to join you?

①

Huh? . . . Oh! . . . Er . . . Gee Nick, I didn't know. I mean I thought you and Lucille were busy.

Yeah, we're busy all right! Waiting to hear from you.

②

MAKING THE WURST OF IT

Bob, I'm a little self-conscious about having you over for supper. I know your mother. She's the greatest cook in the world. Every night your dinner is a many course banquet.

①

I can't compete with your mother when she makes things like **lobster diablo, schnitzer ala Holstein, pheasant under glass, venison** and **filet mignon.**

②

CHAPTER AND WORSE

HOLIDAY DIN

WHAT'S DINE IS MINE

MOM'S THE WORD

HOUSE-BROKEN

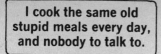

COPELESS CASE

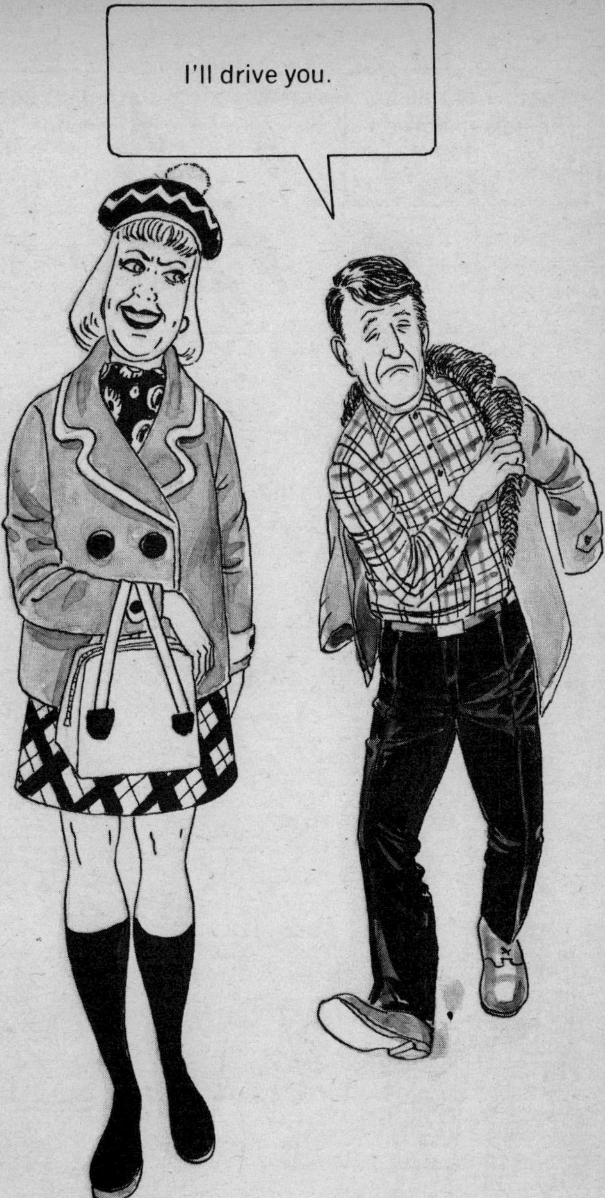
I'll drive you.

PRATTLE FATIGUE

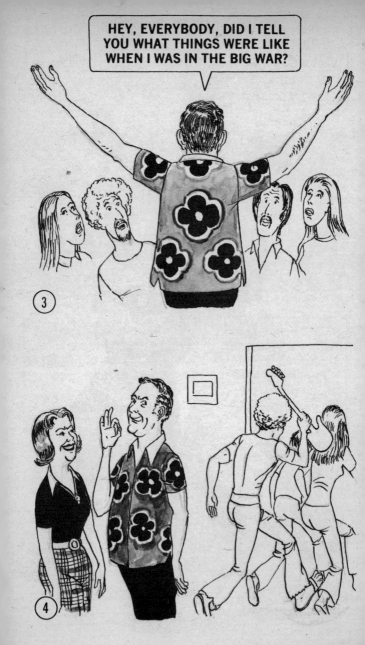

TRASHING IT OUT

MAKING A LIVING

PAIN PAIN GO AWAY

LABOR RELATION

A TRAIN IN THE NECK

That GOD Damn commuter train! It's so darned loused up. Almost every morning it gets me to work late.

Then it goes against my record. You don't know the company I work for. It doesn't do any good explaining.

HAIR SAY

Look at those disgusting kids with their long hair and straggly beards. They call it **DOING THEIR OWN THING.**

①

I say a law should be passed preventing kids from doing their own thing.

②

RARE FORM

ROUTE OF THE TROUBLE

HOME IS WHERE THE TART IS

MOB SEEN

LIVING EXAMPLES

TO YELL AND BACK

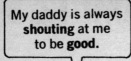

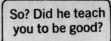

①

②

AGED IN THE WOOD

(1)

(2)

(3)

CIVIL WRONGS

DOLLARS AND SENSE

THE IRE OF THE BEHOLDER

BORN LOOTER

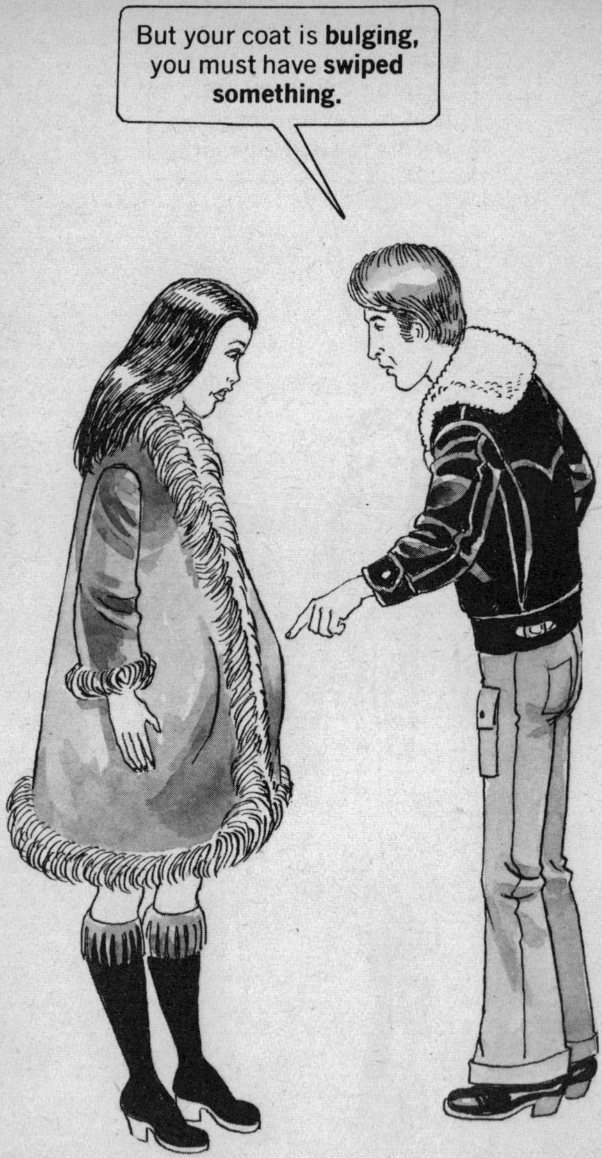
But your coat is **bulging,** you must have **swiped** **something.**

SAILOR'S BEWARE

EGGED ON

SOMETHING'S NOT SO ROTTEN IN DENMARK

WIRE-TRAPPED

ROBBIN' HOODS

DOCUMENTARY EVIDENCE

YOU CALL THIS LIVING?

CURVING HIS APPETITE

And let me tell you, it's **pretty wild . . .** reading and looking at all these pictures.
KRUD
SMUT

SEXSATIONAL

NOTHING IS FOR NOTHING

A TELLING BLOW

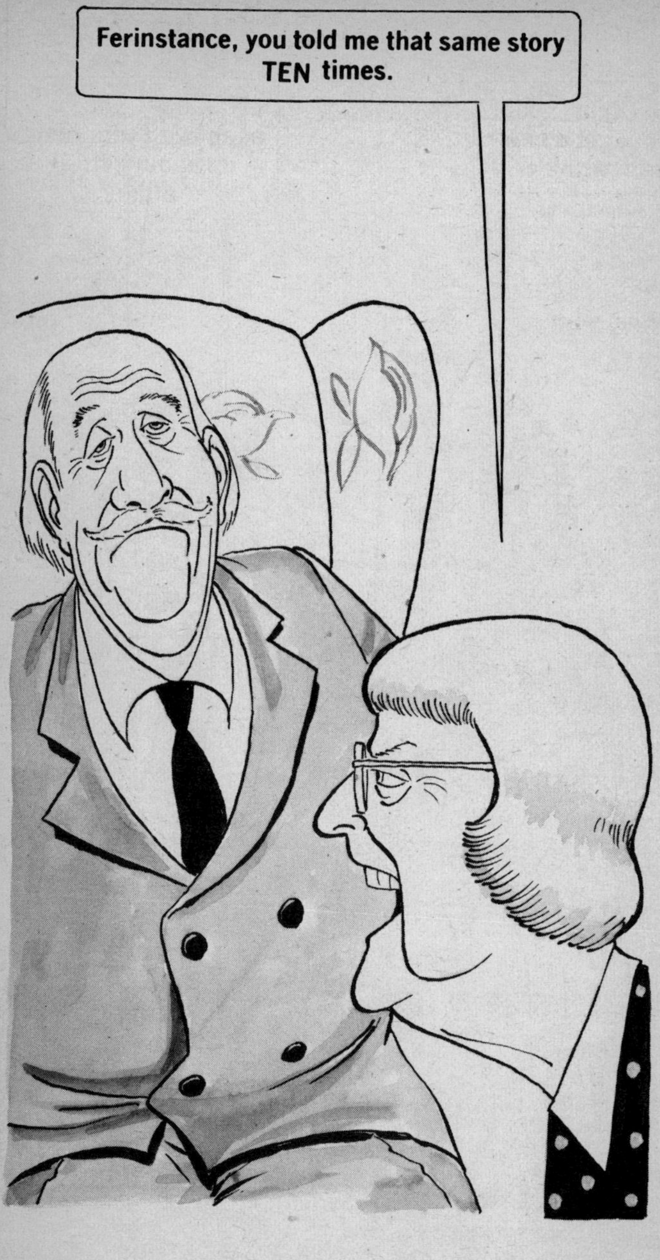
Ferinstance, you told me that same story TEN times.

PERPETUAL NOTION

But the trouble is, the only thing I'm getting better at is worrying about GETTING OLDER.

FROM NAGS TO RICHES

When do I ever stop being **hounded?**

(1)

When I was a kid, my parents hounded and hounded me, "YOU GOTTA MAKE GOOD! YOU GOTTA MAKE GOOD!"

(2)

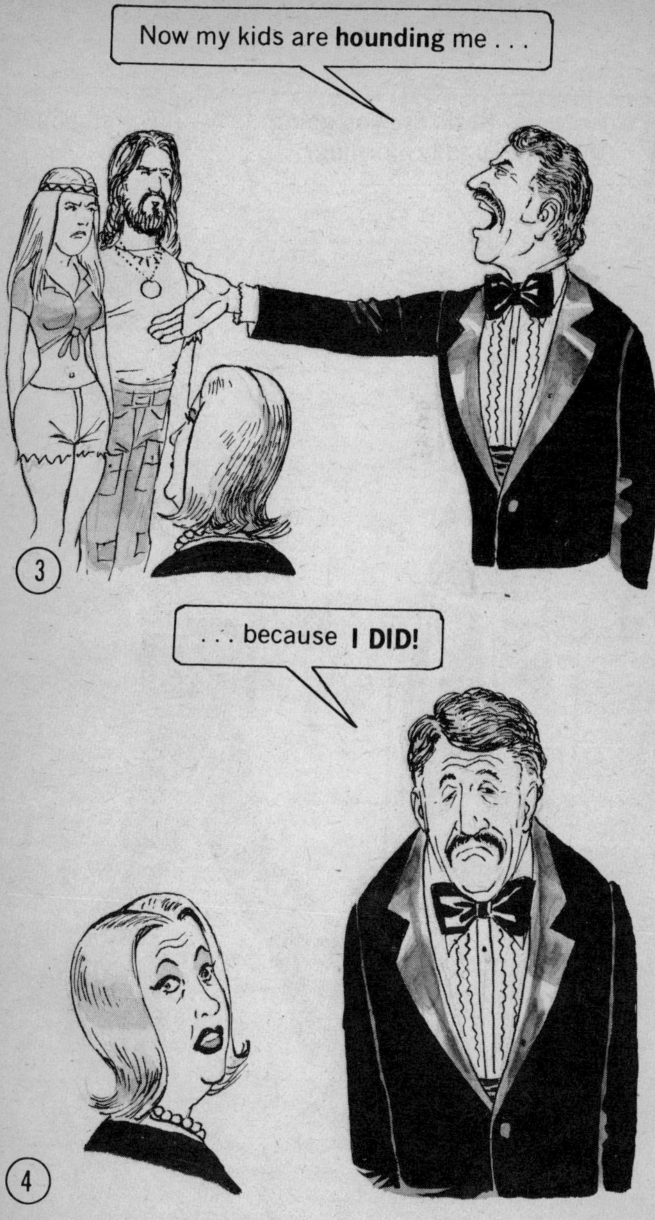
Now my kids are hounding me . . .
3
. . . because I DID!
4

GOD'S LITTLE ACHERS

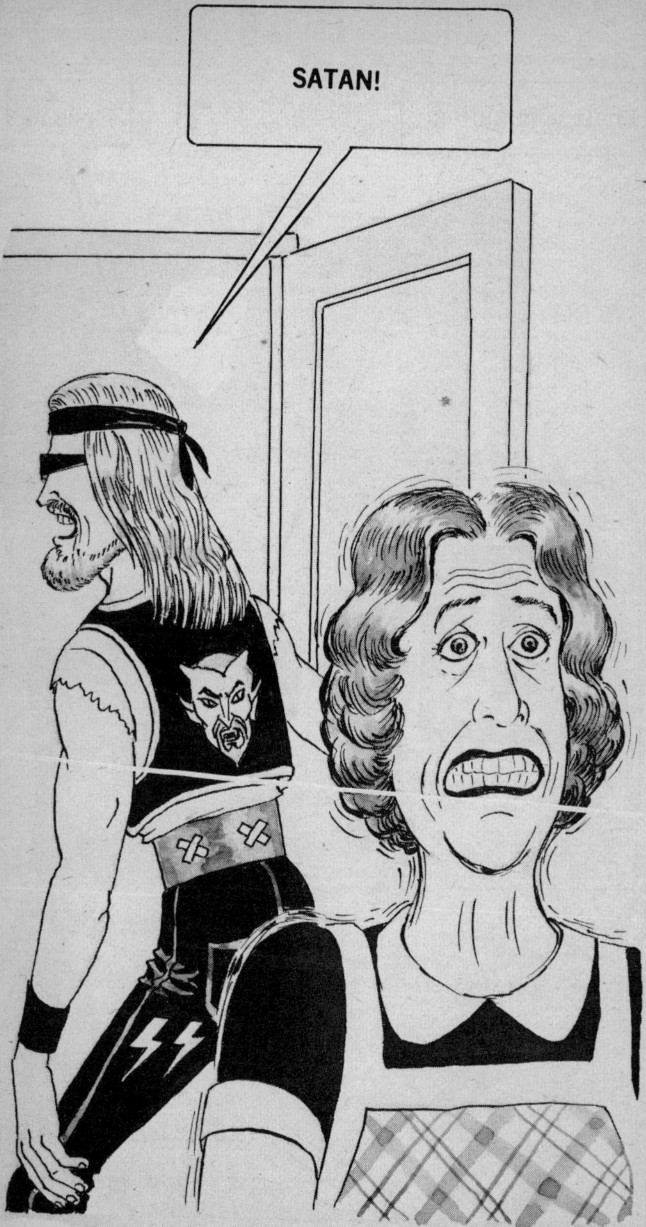
SATAN!

RAIL SPLITTER

MASTER PLAN

HAIRLINE FRACTURE

Dave Berg

LOOKS AT PEOPLE

AT YOUR BOOK DEALERS NOW!

ONLY 75c